D0917936

COLORFUL
ORIGAMI

by Toyoaki Kawai
translated by Thomas I. Elliott
edited by Don Kenny

BARNES & NOBLE BOOKS

A DIVISION OF HARPER & ROW, PUBLISHERS

New York, Cambridge, Philadelphia

San Francisco, London, Mexico City

São Paulo, Sydney

Published by Ottenheimer Publishers, Inc.
Exclusively distributed by Barnes & Noble, a
division of Harper & Row, Publishers, Inc.,
New York, New York 10022

Contents

(Bold numbers indicate color plates ; other numbers indicate pages showing paper-folding sequences.)

Basic folds

Cover Photo: Female Demon's Mask and Small Crane

COLORFUL ORIGAMI

by Toyoaki Kawai
translated by Thomas I. Elliott
edited by Don Kenny

2nd Printing 1986

Copyright © 1970 by Hoikusha Publishing Co., Ltd.
Copyright © 1983 by Ottenheimer Publishers, Inc.

INTRODUCTION

Origami, paper-folding, can be enjoyed by children and adults alike. The forms I introduce in this book derive from basic patterns transmitted in Japan for perhaps a thousand years.

As a traditional art, origami has permeated deeply into everyday life in Japan and helped form the versatility and creativity so many Japanese possess. I hope that origami will continue to occupy a niche in the lives of future generations of non-Japanese as well as Japan.

Is there a child who will not sit entranced as his mother's hands move swiftly, strangely, to create an elephant, a rose, a spaceship, or other favorite animal or object? Kindergarten teachers recognize that children feel a strange attraction toward origami and make origami zoos and botany gardens filled with paper animals and flowers. The paper creations not only help initiate a happy dialogue between children and teachers but also decorate the kindergarten rooms.

To practice origami requires only paper and a little time. Whether devotee or novice, therefore, one may enjoy the origami art in every conceivable situation. While travelling, origami is ideal for passing time alone or sharing pleasant moments with companions. Some people fold origami while commuting.

People are especially delighted when presented an origami work created before their eyes. The traveller who takes origami techniques home from Japan carries one of the finest possible souvenirs, and an art that is close to all Japanese hearts.

Origami zoo

Gorilla

The basic hat fold is used for gorilla, rocket and sombrero.

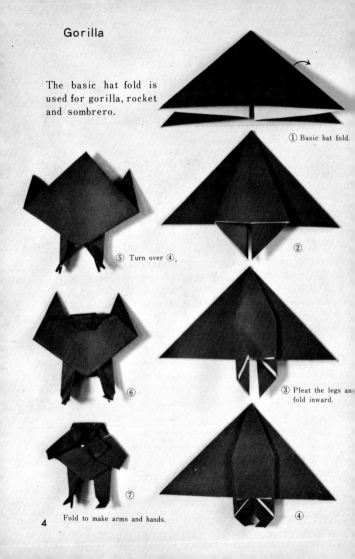

① Basic hat fold.

②

⑤ Turn over ④.

③ Pleat the legs an fold inward.

⑥

⑦

Fold to make arms and hands.

④

4

Camel

(two sheets of paper necessary)

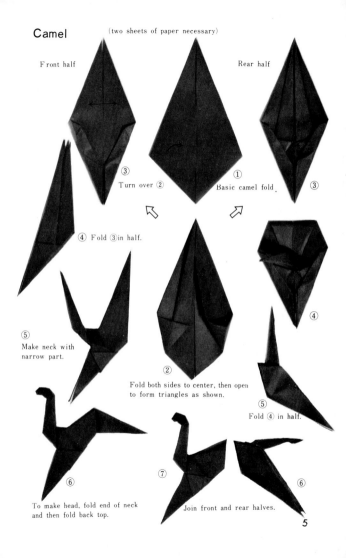

Front half

Rear half

③ Turn over ②

① Basic camel fold.

③

④ Fold ③ in half.

⑤ Make neck with narrow part.

④

② Fold both sides to center, then open to form triangles as shown.

⑤ Fold ④ in half.

⑥ To make head, fold end of neck and then fold back top.

⑦ Join front and rear halves.

⑥

5

The baby kangaroo requires paper
one-quarter the size of that needed
for the grown kangaroo. Two-colored paper was used for the jumping pony;(folding sequence on p.101)
roughtextured paper was used for
the kangaroo.

Kangaroo

Jumping pony

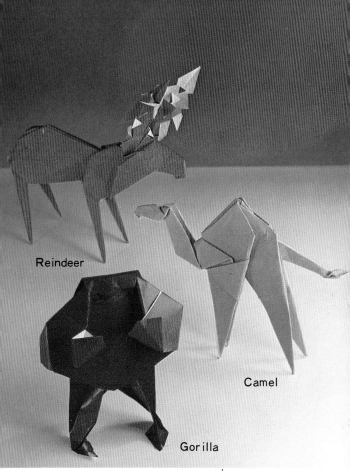

Reindeer

Camel

Gorilla

Try to make a double-humped camel. If you use slightly stiffer paper for the reindeer its antlers will not droop. Use your ingenuity to make a running reindeer.

7

Kangaroo

Same process for adult or baby kangaroo. Latter uses 1/4 size paper. Scissors used to form ears and front legs.

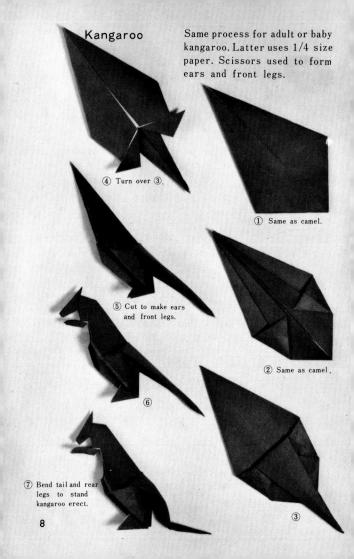

④ Turn over ③.

① Same as camel.

⑤ Cut to make ears and front legs.

② Same as camel.

⑥

⑦ Bend tail and rear legs to stand kangaroo erect.

③

8

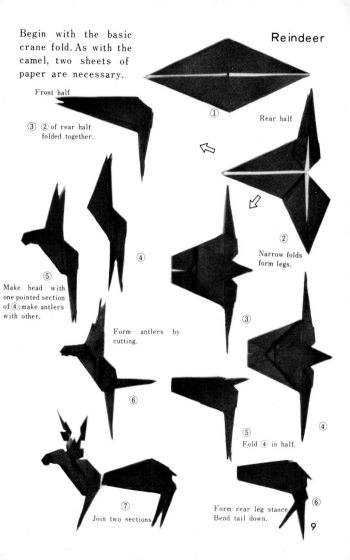

Begin with the basic crane fold. As with the camel, two sheets of paper are necessary.

Reindeer

① Rear half

Front half

③ ② of rear half folded together.

② Narrow folds form legs.

④

③

⑤ Make head with one pointed section of ④; make antlers with other.

④

Form antlers by cutting.

⑥

⑤ Fold ④ in half.

⑦ Join two sections

⑥ Form rear leg stance. Bend tail down.

9

Giraffe

Elephant

Horse   Pay close attention to leg angles when joining front and rear. Experiment with various stances.
(folding sequence on p. 98)

Giraffe

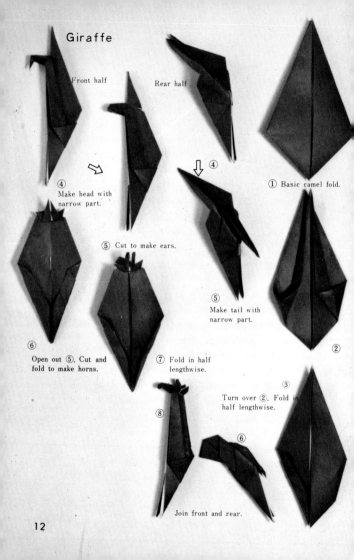

Front half

Rear half

① Basic camel fold.

④

④

Make head with narrow part.

⑤ Cut to make ears.

⑤ Make tail with narrow part.

②

⑥ Open out ⑤. Cut and fold to make horns.

⑦ Fold in half lengthwise.

Turn over ②. Fold in half lengthwise.

③

⑧

⑥

Join front and rear.

Elephant

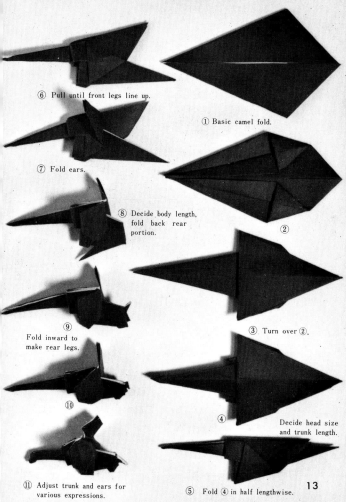

⑥ Pull until front legs line up.

① Basic camel fold.

⑦ Fold ears.

⑧ Decide body length, fold back rear portion.

②

⑨
Fold inward to make rear legs.

③ Turn over ②.

⑩

④

Decide head size and trunk length.

⑪ Adjust trunk and ears for various expressions.

⑤ Fold ④ in half lengthwise.

Dinosaur   Snake
(folding sequence on p.103)

Turtle (folding sequence on p.100)

Rabbit

Snake

Snakes are easy to fold. Practice having snake raise its head while coiled.

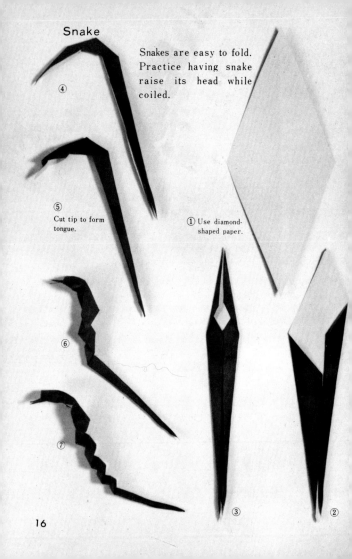

④

⑤ Cut tip to form tongue.

① Use diamond-shaped paper.

⑥

⑦

③

②

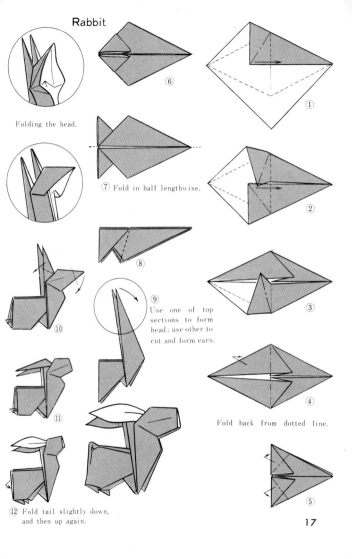

Rabbit

Folding the head.

⑥

⑦ Fold in half lengthwise.

①

②

⑧

③

⑨ Use one of top sections to form head; use other to cut and form ears.

④

Fold back from dotted line.

⑩

⑪

⑤

⑫ Fold tail slightly down, and then up again.

17

Goldfish

Ray
(folding sequence on p.102)

Carp

Goldfish

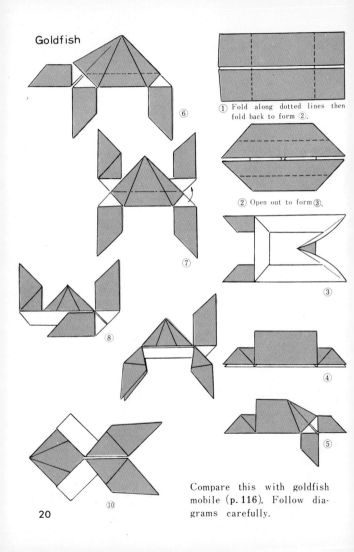

① Fold along dotted lines then fold back to form ②.

② Open out to form ③.

③

④

⑤

⑥

⑦

⑧

⑩

20

Compare this with goldfish mobile (p. 116). Follow diagrams carefully.

Carp

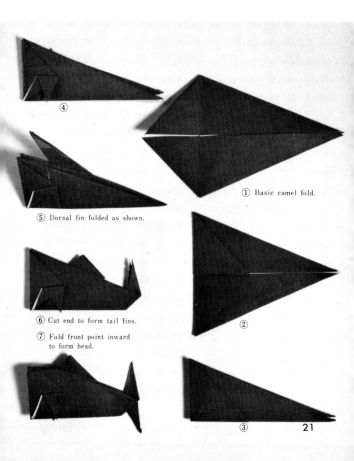

① Basic camel fold.

④

⑤ Dorsal fin folded as shown.

⑥ Cut end to form tail fins.

⑦ Fold front point inward to form head.

②

③

21

Origami
aviary

Raven

⑤ Begin at ④ of adult raven. Fold top triangle down.

⑥

⑦

⑧

⑨

⑩

The heads and legs of all birds are folded similarly. Compare your adult and young ravens closely. Great pleasure is gained when one creates lifelike animals from sheets of paper. It is a pleasure often forgotten in busy, modern life. Folding origami is refreshing and helps one to recall the simple joys that children experience. Origami also helps to develop creativity in children, and stimulates their interest in their surroundings.

24

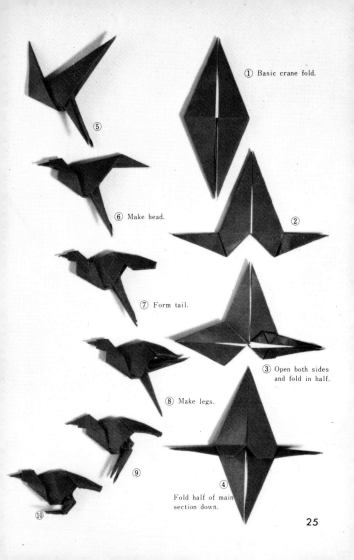

① Basic crane fold.

②

③ Open both sides and fold in half.

④ Fold half of main section down.

⑤

⑥ Make head.

⑦ Form tail.

⑧ Make legs.

⑨

⑩

25

Swan
(folding sequence on p.105)

Flamingo

Standing crane

Raven   A baby raven needs one-quarter the paper required for an adult raven. Attend closely to the shape of the raven's body.

◀ The crane fold is complicated, and an adhesive is probably necessary.

27

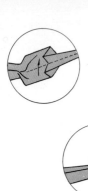

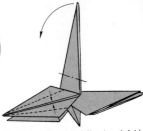

⑨ Open left portion (legs) and fold back along dotted lines. Open neck part and fold down.

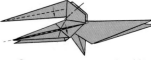

⑩ Fold neck in half along dotted line. Bring legs together again.

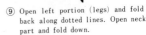

⑪ Turn back neck in direction of arrow.

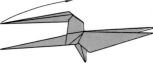

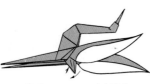

⑬ Open wings, and fold down tail.

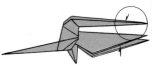

⑫ Refer to insets to form head.

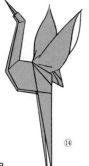

⑭

28

Standing crane

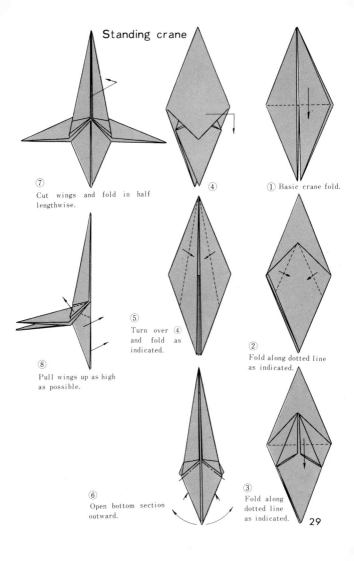

⑦ Cut wings and fold in half lengthwise.

④

① Basic crane fold.

⑤ Turn over ④ and fold as indicated.

② Fold along dotted line as indicated.

⑧ Pull wings up as high as possible.

③ Fold along dotted line as indicated.

⑥ Open bottom section outward.

29

Java sparrow (folding sequence on p.106)

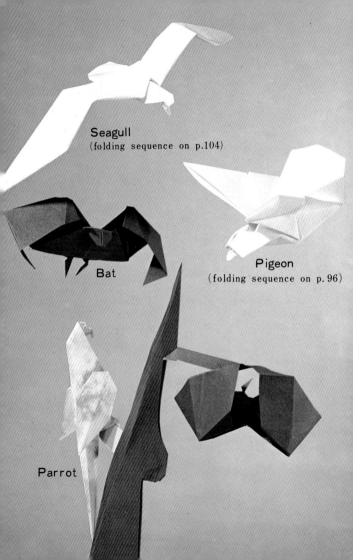

Seagull
(folding sequence on p.104)

Bat

Pigeon
(folding sequence on p. 96)

Parrot

Bat

As with parrot, begin with an isosceles triangle. The easiest way to prepare the triangle is to cut a piece of square paper diagonally in half.

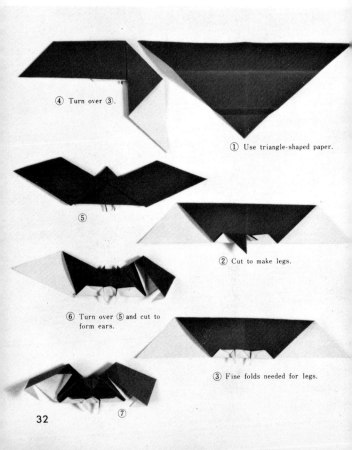

④ Turn over ③.

① Use triangle-shaped paper.

⑤

② Cut to make legs.

⑥ Turn over ⑤ and cut to form ears.

③ Fine folds needed for legs.

32   ⑦

Parrot

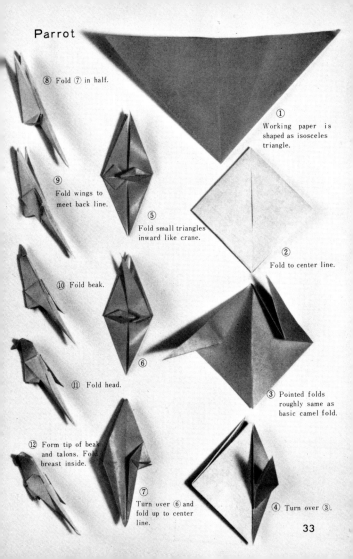

⑧ Fold ⑦ in half.

① Working paper is shaped as isosceles triangle.

⑨ Fold wings to meet back line.

⑤ Fold small triangles inward like crane.

② Fold to center line.

⑩ Fold beak.

⑥

⑪ Fold head.

③ Pointed folds roughly same as basic camel fold.

⑫ Form tip of beak and talons. Fold breast inside.

⑦ Turn over ⑥ and fold up to center line.

④ Turn over ③.

33

Bird in flight

With two-colored paper you can obtain color variations by folding one time from one side and the next time from the other side.

(folding sequence on p.109)

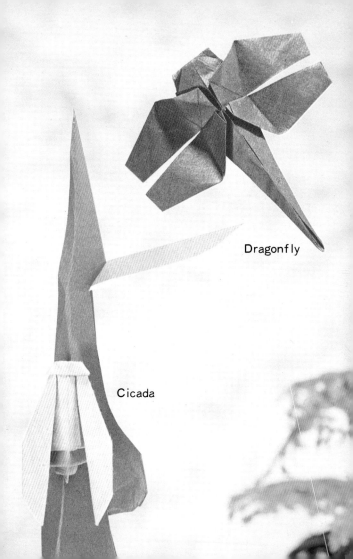

Dragonfly

Cicada

Cicada

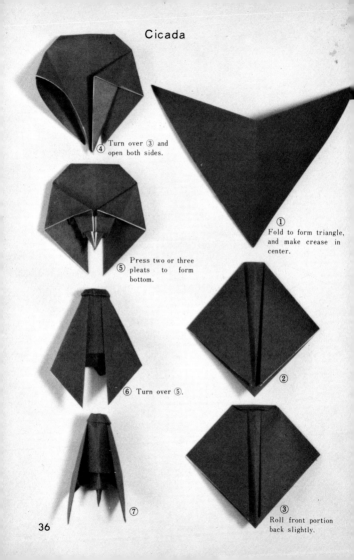

④ Turn over ③ and open both sides.

⑤ Press two or three pleats to form bottom.

⑥ Turn over ⑤.

⑦

① Fold to form triangle, and make crease in center.

②

③ Roll front portion back slightly.

36

Dragonfly

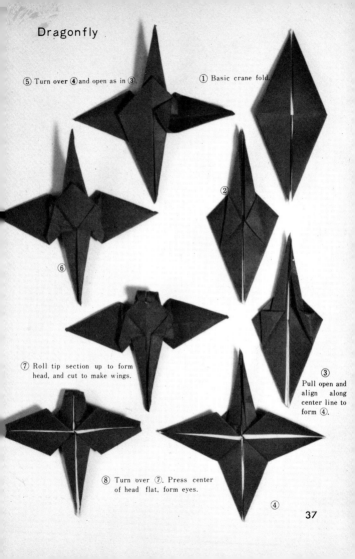

⑤ Turn over ④ and open as in ③.

① Basic crane fold.

②

⑥

⑦ Roll tip section up to form head, and cut to make wings.

③ Pull open and align along center line to form ④.

⑧ Turn over ⑦. Press center of head flat, form eyes.

④

37

Be especially careful not to tear petals when folding. Use soft paper.

Water lily
(folding sequence on p.111)

Frog

Camellia   Use only slight pressure when folding
to give the camellia edges their proper
shape. More striking results are achieved
with two-colored paper.

Camellia

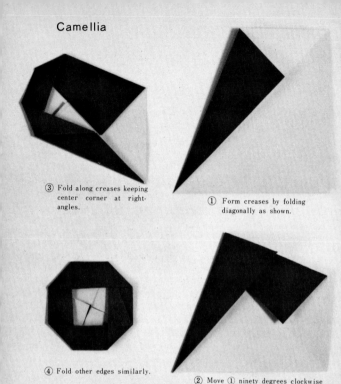

③ Fold along creases keeping center corner at right-angles.

① Form creases by folding diagonally as shown.

④ Fold other edges similarly.

② Move ① ninety degrees clockwise and fold next corner.

The camellia is one of the easiest origami flowers to make. The creases made in ① helped in steps ③ and ④. Fold so that one crease touches another crease. Creases often play an important role in origami.

Frog

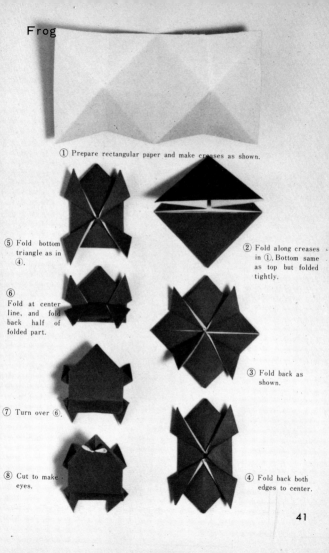

① Prepare rectangular paper and make creases as shown.

⑤ Fold bottom triangle as in ④.

⑥ Fold at center line, and fold back half of folded part.

② Fold along creases in ①. Bottom same as top but folded tightly.

⑦ Turn over ⑥.

③ Fold back as shown.

⑧ Cut to make eyes.

④ Fold back both edges to center.

41

Iris   (folding sequence on p.110)

Broad bellflower   Lily

Broad bellflower

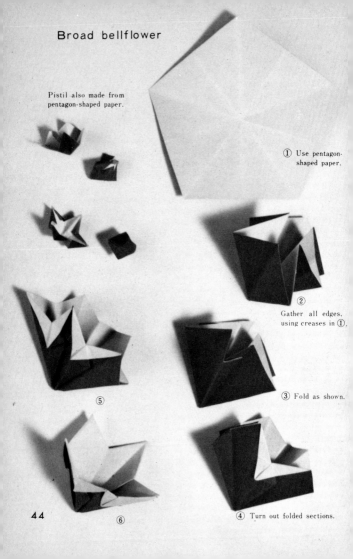

Pistil also made from pentagon-shaped paper.

① Use pentagon-shaped paper.

② Gather all edges, using creases in ①.

③ Fold as shown.

④ Turn out folded sections.

⑤

⑥

44

Lily

Two triangular sheets of paper are folded separately and joined to form the lily.

⑤ Fold inward along creases.

④ Make creases.

① Equilateral triangle.

⑥ Open and then fold bottom part to make it narrow. Two sheets of paper placed one on the other and refolded along creases.

⑦

Bring bottom left corner to top of triangle to make crease. Repeat with bottom right corner. ②

⑧

⑨ Roll petal tips down for effect.

③ Fold to top, open folds, and push flat.

Hydrangea parts are pasted on a foundation about the size of a fist. The snail's head may give you some trouble.

Snail

Hydrangea

White flower

Make many small flowers and glue them on branches to gain the best effect.

White flower

④

① Fold in four.

⑤

②

⑥

③

48

Hydrangea

Hydrangea is an aggregate flower. Many flowers set together make one hydrangea. The folds are complicated from step ⑦ on, so study the illustrations closely.

① Basic pony fold.

②

③

④

⑤

⑥

⑦ Turn over ⑥

⑧

⑨

⑩

⑪

49

Butterfly

Caterpillar

Foliage plant   Use glossy paper.

Foliage plant

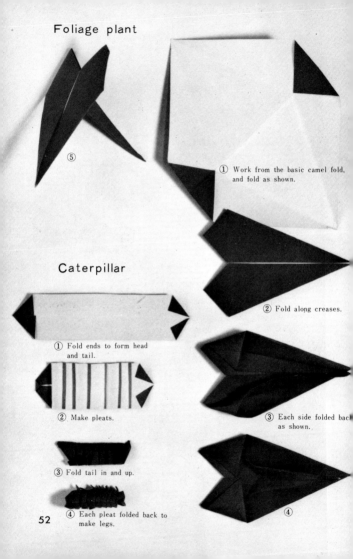

⑤

① Work from the basic camel fold, and fold as shown.

② Fold along creases.

③ Each side folded back as shown.

④

Caterpillar

① Fold ends to form head and tail.

② Make pleats.

③ Fold tail in and up.

52

④ Each pleat folded back to make legs.

Butterfly

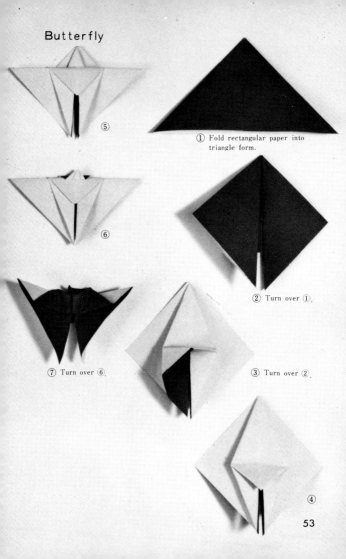

⑤

① Fold rectangular paper into triangle form.

⑥

② Turn over ①.

⑦ Turn over ⑥.

③ Turn over ②.

④

53

Jet plane

Rocket
(folding sequence on p.113)

Kite

Colorful varieties of kites depend
on whether you fold from the front
or the back. Try to alternate.

Jet plane

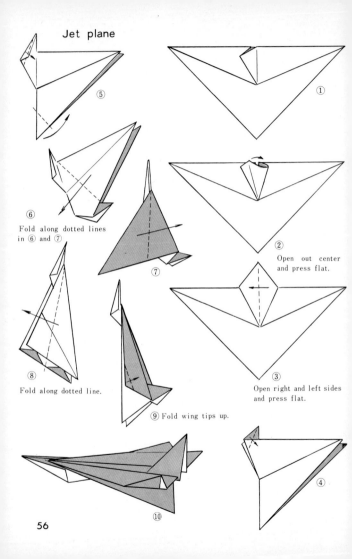

①

② Open out center and press flat.

③ Open right and left sides and press flat.

④

⑤

⑥ Fold along dotted lines in ⑥ and ⑦

⑦

⑧ Fold along dotted line.

⑨ Fold wing tips up.

⑩

56

Kite

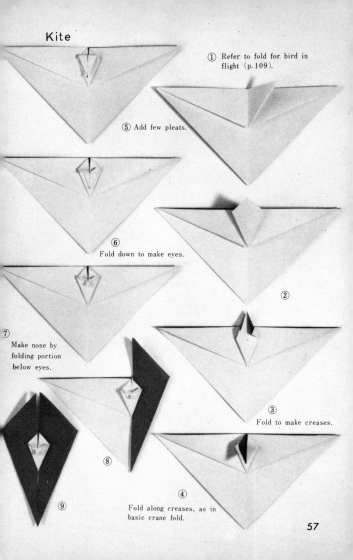

① Refer to fold for bird in flight (p. 109).

⑤ Add few pleats.

⑥ Fold down to make eyes.

②

③ Fold to make creases.

⑦ Make nose by folding portion below eyes.

⑧

④ Fold along creases, as in basic crane fold.

⑨

57

Wall decoration

Standing baby

Sitting baby

Crawling baby
(folding sequences for babies on p.114)

Crane-shaped receptacle
(folding sequence on p.112)

Pigeon-shaped receptacle

Crawling baby

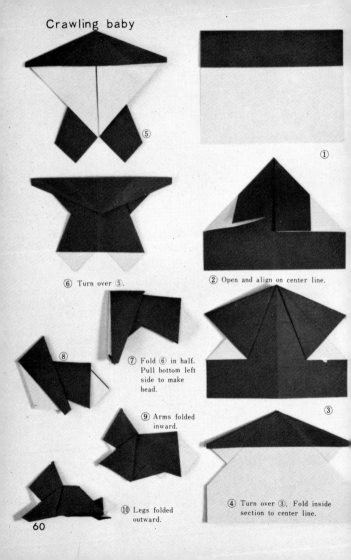

①

② Open and align on center line.

③

④ Turn over ③. Fold inside section to center line.

⑤

⑥ Turn over ⑤.

⑦ Fold ⑥ in half. Pull bottom left side to make head.

⑧

⑨ Arms folded inward.

⑩ Legs folded outward.

60

⑤ Open and align on center line.

⑥

⑦

⑧ Open to make bottom of box.

⑨

①

② Fold back and open triangular part.

③

④ Fold as in basic crane fold.

61

Hanging ornaments

(folding sequence

on p.117)

The camellia provides the basic fold for the ornamental ball. If you intend to use this as a lampshade do not use flammable material.

Use paper with colorful patterns or wrapping paper.

Table mat

Card case

Card case

① Fold in half.

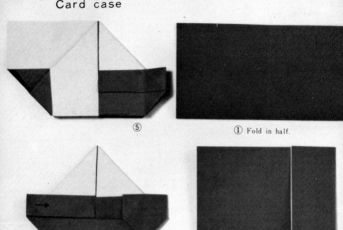
② Fold right side to center.

③ Fold left side to center and open right side as shown.

④ Fold top of right side to center line as shown. Open small triangle.

⑤

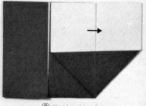
⑥ Fold back.

⑦ Fold top layer triangle down and tuck inside.

⑧

64

Mat

Make numerous mats and join them together to form various shapes.

① Cut as shown.

④

⑤

②

③

⑥ Join mats by opening triangular sections on back and sliding them into next mats.

Bamboo boat

The bamboo boat can be a simple decoration or a mobile.

Small box

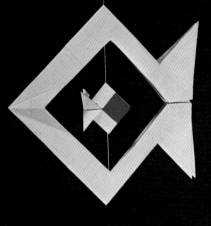

Goldfish mobile

Lantern

The small goldfish can be made using the cut-out section. (folding sequence on p.116)

Lantern

⑥

③

①

Basic pony fold.

⑦

④

⑧

⑨ Join six of these to form lantern.

②

⑤

Use as hanging decoration or lampshade. Do not use combustible material next to lighted bulb.

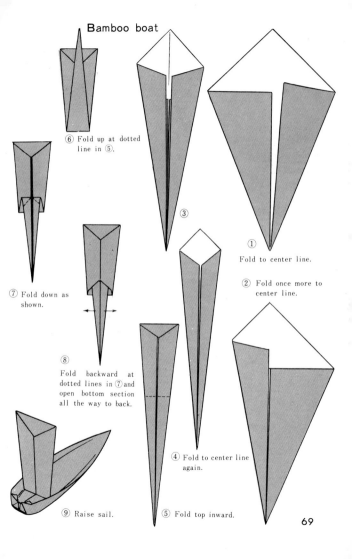

Bamboo boat

⑥ Fold up at dotted line in ⑤.

③

① Fold to center line.

② Fold once more to center line.

⑦ Fold down as shown.

⑧ Fold backward at dotted lines in ⑦ and open bottom section all the way to back.

④ Fold to center line again.

⑤ Fold top inward.

⑨ Raise sail.

69

Samurai helmet

With the helmet, different colors give quite different effects. I used the same paper for the costume and the helmet.

Noh costume

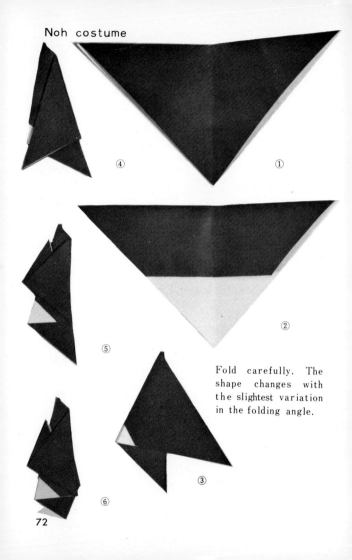

Noh costume

① ② ③ ④ ⑤ ⑥

Fold carefully. The
shape changes with
the slightest variation
in the folding angle.

72

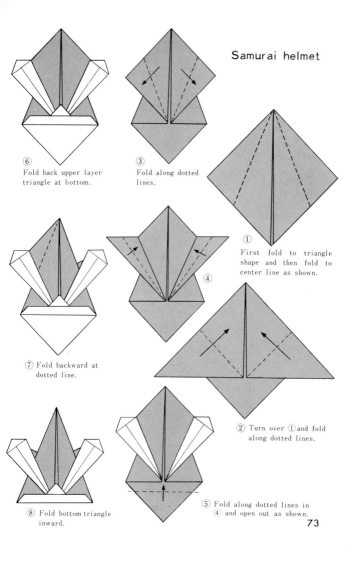

Samurai helmet

⑥ Fold back upper layer triangle at bottom.

③ Fold along dotted lines.

① First fold to triangle shape and then fold to center line as shown.

④

⑦ Fold backward at dotted line.

② Turn over ① and fold along dotted lines.

⑧ Fold bottom triangle inward.

⑤ Fold along dotted lines in ④ and open out as shown.

73

Girls' Day dolls

Use as colorful paper as available. Add crowns, fans, and other accessories to give realistic effect.

Girls' Day dolls

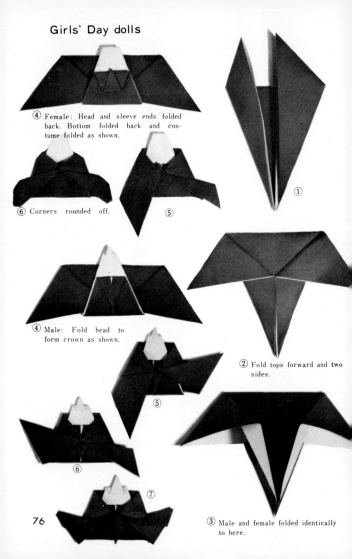

④ Female: Head and sleeve ends folded back. Bottom folded back and costume folded as shown.

⑥ Corners rounded off.

⑤

①

④ Male: Fold head to form crown as shown.

⑤

② Fold tops forward and two sides.

⑥

⑦

③ Male and female folded identically to here.

76

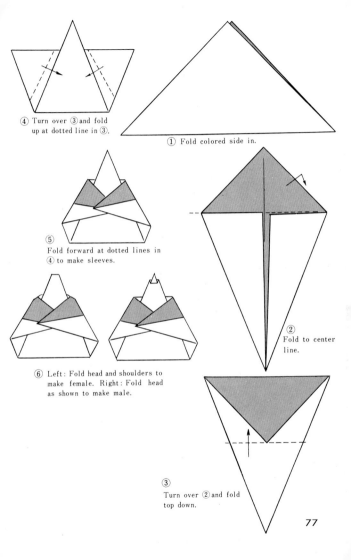

④ Turn over ③ and fold up at dotted line in ③.

① Fold colored side in.

⑤ Fold forward at dotted lines in ④ to make sleeves.

② Fold to center line.

⑥ Left: Fold head and shoulders to make female. Right: Fold head as shown to make male.

③ Turn over ② and fold top down.

77

Hat

Paper about two feet square will give you a hat large enough for an adult.

Sombrero

Hat

⑤ Roll back along sides.

① Fold in half.

⑥

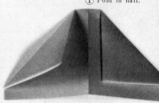

② Open triangles on sides and press flat.

⑦ Form brim.

③ Fold back opened sections at center lines.

⑧ Curl brim edge in at top.

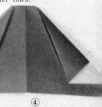

④

Sombrero

Basic hat fold.

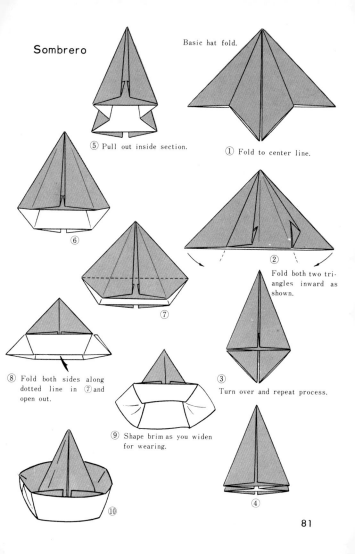

⑤ Pull out inside section.

① Fold to center line.

⑥

② Fold both two triangles inward as shown.

⑦

③ Turn over and repeat process.

⑧ Fold both sides along dotted line in ⑦ and open out.

⑨ Shape brim as you widen for wearing.

④

⑩

Devil's mask

Old man's mask

"Deija" devil's mask

Female demon's mask

Facial expression can be changed depending on individual taste.

83

Old man's mask

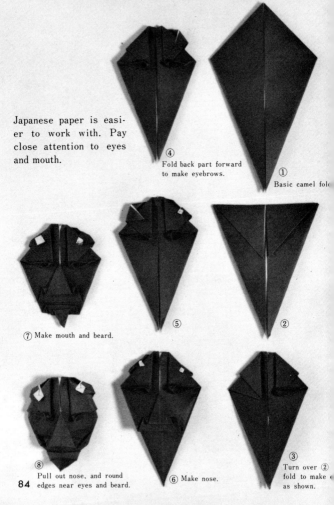

Japanese paper is easier to work with. Pay close attention to eyes and mouth.

④ Fold back part forward to make eyebrows.

① Basic camel fold

⑦ Make mouth and beard.

⑤

②

⑧ Pull out nose, and round edges near eyes and beard.

⑥ Make nose.

③ Turn over ② fold to make e as shown.

Female demon's mask

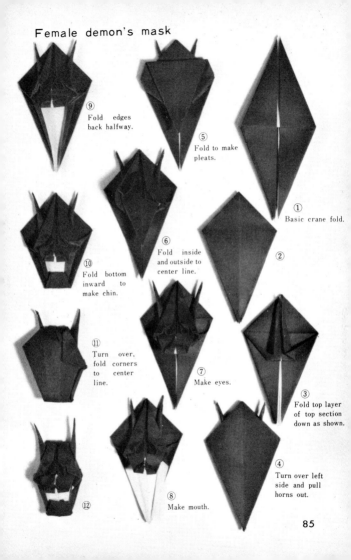

① Basic crane fold.

②

③ Fold top layer of top section down as shown.

④ Turn over left side and pull horns out.

⑤ Fold to make pleats.

⑥ Fold inside and outside to center line.

⑦ Make eyes.

⑧ Make mouth.

⑨ Fold edges back halfway.

⑩ Fold bottom inward to make chin.

⑪ Turn over, fold corners to center line.

⑫

Buddha's mask   Golden ghost's mask

Mask for Chinese opera

I have tried to approximate the genuine masks.

Mask for Chinese opera

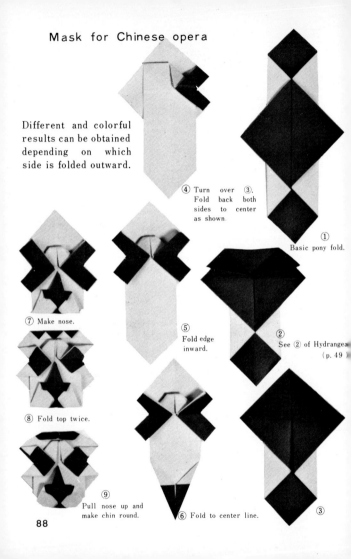

Different and colorful
results can be obtained
depending on which
side is folded outward.

④ Turn over ③.
Fold back both
sides to center
as shown.

①
Basic pony fold.

②
See ② of Hydrangea
(p. 49)

③

⑦ Make nose.

⑤
Fold edge
inward.

⑧ Fold top twice.

⑨
Pull nose up and
make chin round.

⑥ Fold to center line.

Buddha's mask

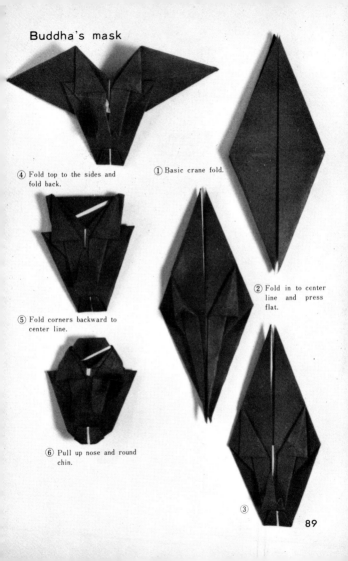

④ Fold top to the sides and fold back.

① Basic crane fold.

② Fold in to center line and press flat.

⑤ Fold corners backward to center line.

⑥ Pull up nose and round chin.

③

89

Red and black mask   Two-faced mask

The red and black mask uses two different
colors folded back to back.

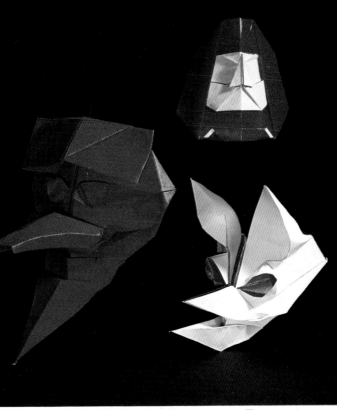

Long-nosed goblin Daruma Fox mask

(folding sequence
on p.118)

Experiment with Daruma's costume for different
color effects and facial expression.

91

Red and black mask

④ Fold along center line.

⑤ Fold as shown.

⑦

⑧ Make eyes.

⑨ Make nose.

⑩ Pull up nose, make chin round.

①

②

③

⑥

92

Daruma (Two sheets of paper needed)

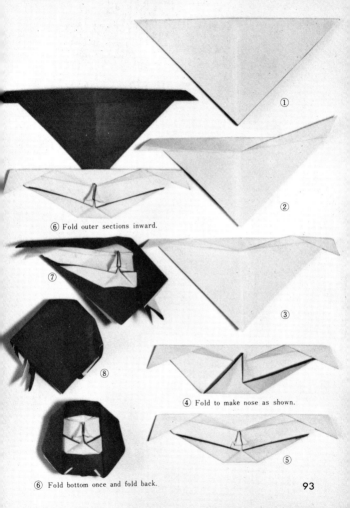

①

②

⑥ Fold outer sections inward.

⑦

③

⑧

④ Fold to make nose as shown.

⑤

⑥ Fold bottom once and fold back.

93

Pigeons in flight

These pigeons in flight decorated a corner of the Livelihood Industry Pavilion at EXPO'70. Electricity is used to make them flap their wings as if they were flying. This sort of decoration is ideal for a child's room.

Pigeon in flight

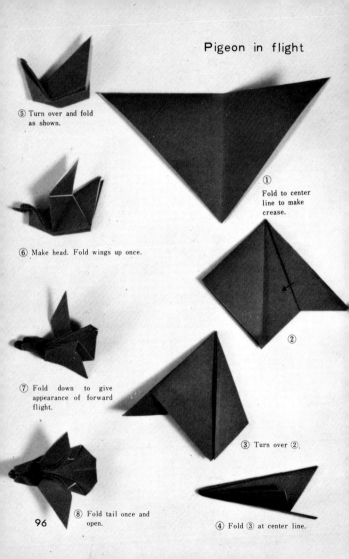

① Fold to center line to make crease.

②

③ Turn over ②.

④ Fold ③ at center line.

⑤ Turn over and fold as shown.

⑥ Make head. Fold wings up once.

⑦ Fold down to give appearance of forward flight.

⑧ Fold tail once and open.

96

Color plates for the following origami figures
appeared earlier in the book.
(See the Table of Contents.)

Horse

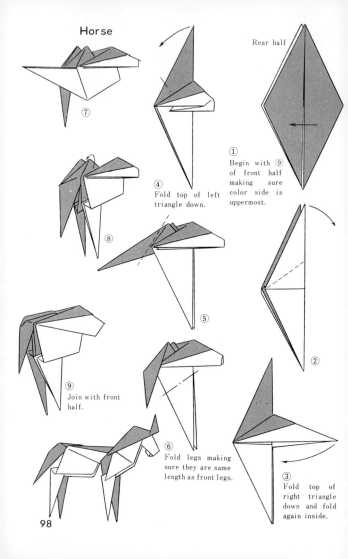

⑦

Rear half

① Begin with ⑨ of front half making sure color side is uppermost.

④ Fold top of left triangle down.

⑧

②

⑤

⑨ Join with front half.

⑥ Fold legs making sure they are same length as front legs.

③ Fold top of right triangle down and fold again inside.

98

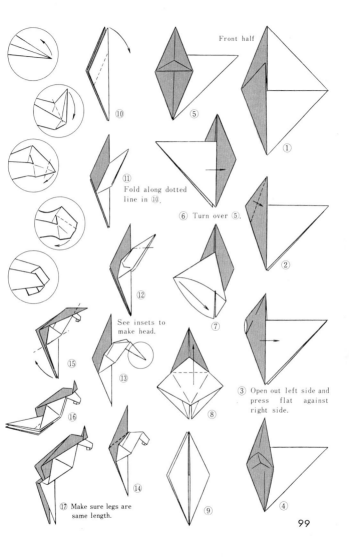

Front half

⑤

①

②

③ Open out left side and press flat against right side.

④

⑥ Turn over ⑤.

⑦

⑧

⑨

⑩

⑪ Fold along dotted line in ⑩.

⑫

⑬ See insets to make head.

⑭

⑮

⑯

⑰ Make sure legs are same length.

Turtle

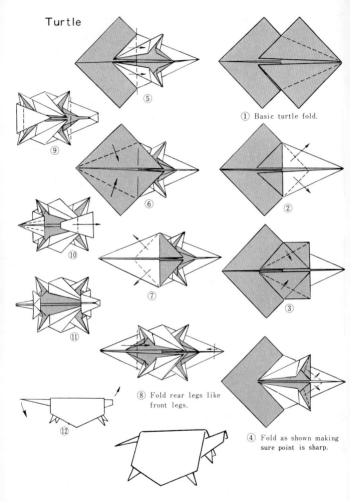

⑤

⑨

① Basic turtle fold.

⑥

②

⑩

③

⑪

⑦

⑧ Fold rear legs like front legs.

④ Fold as shown making sure point is sharp.

⑫

100

Jumping pony

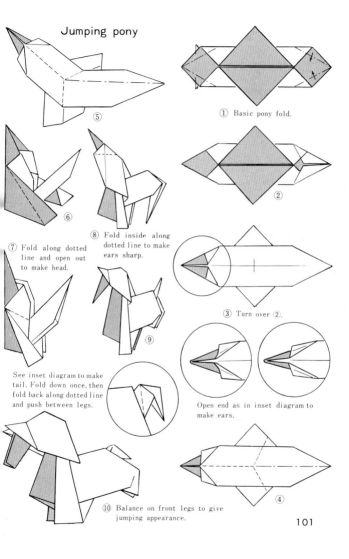

⑤

① Basic pony fold.

②

③ Turn over ②.

Open end as in inset diagram to make ears.

⑥

⑦ Fold along dotted line and open out to make head.

⑧ Fold inside along dotted line to make ears sharp.

⑨

See inset diagram to make tail. Fold down once, then fold back along dotted line and push between legs.

④

⑩ Balance on front legs to give jumping appearance.

101

Ray

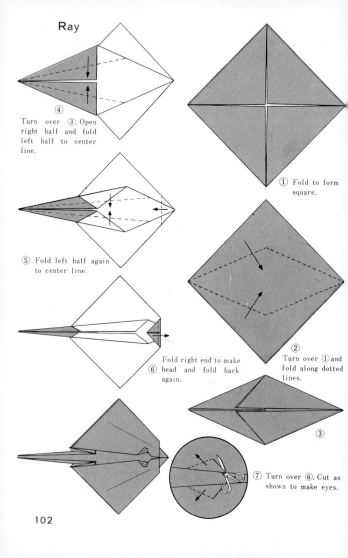

④ Turn over ③. Open right half and fold left half to center line.

⑤ Fold left half again to center line.

⑥ Fold right end to make head and fold back again.

① Fold to form square.

② Turn over ① and fold along dotted lines.

③

⑦ Turn over ⑥. Cut as shown to make eyes.

102

Dinosaur

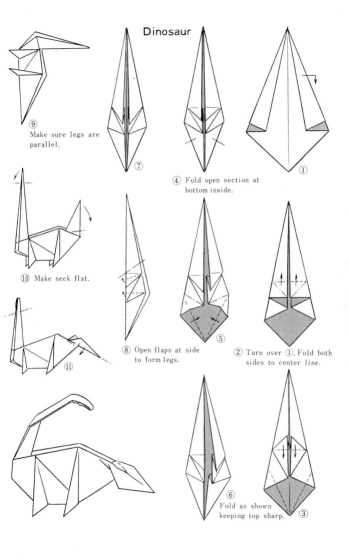

⑨ Make sure legs are parallel.

⑩ Make neck flat.

⑪

⑦

④ Fold open section at bottom inside.

①

⑧ Open flaps at side to form legs.

⑤

② Turn over ①. Fold both sides to center line.

⑥ Fold as shown keeping top sharp.

③

Seagull

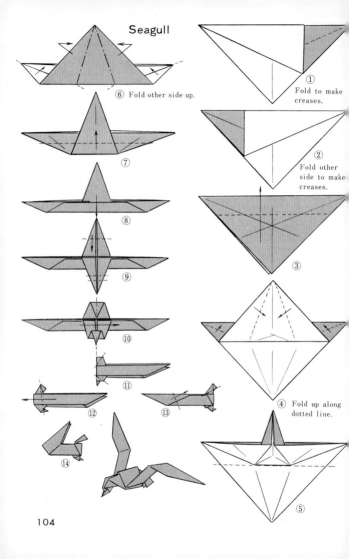

① Fold to make creases.

② Fold other side to make creases.

③

④ Fold up along dotted line.

⑤

⑥ Fold other side up.

⑦

⑧

⑨

⑩

⑪

⑫

⑬

⑭

104

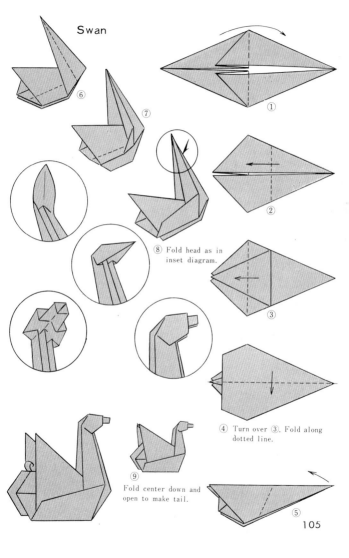

Swan

①

②

③

④ Turn over ③. Fold along dotted line.

⑤

⑥

⑦

⑧ Fold head as in inset diagram.

⑨ Fold center down and open to make tail.

105

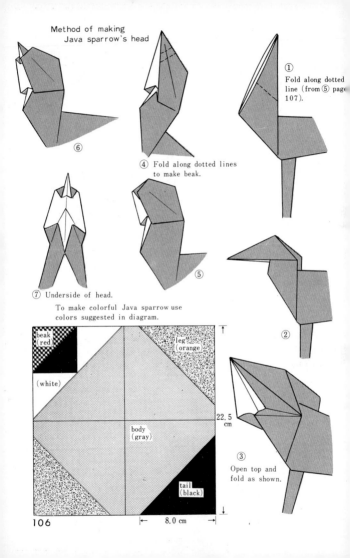

Method of making
    Java sparrow's head

⑥

④ Fold along dotted lines
   to make beak.

⑤

⑦ Underside of head.

To make colorful Java sparrow use
colors suggested in diagram.

① Fold along dotted
   line (from ⑤ page
   107).

②

③

Open top and
fold as shown.

beak
(red)

(white)

leg
(orange)

body
(gray)

tail
(black)

22.5
cm

8.0 cm

106

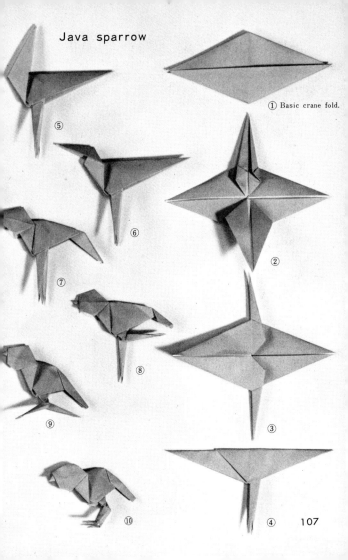

Java sparrow

① Basic crane fold.

⑤

⑥

⑦

②

⑧

③

⑨

④ 107

⑩

Snail

Method of making head

① ① ② ② ③ ④ ⑤ ⑤ ⑥ ⑥ ⑦ ③ ④

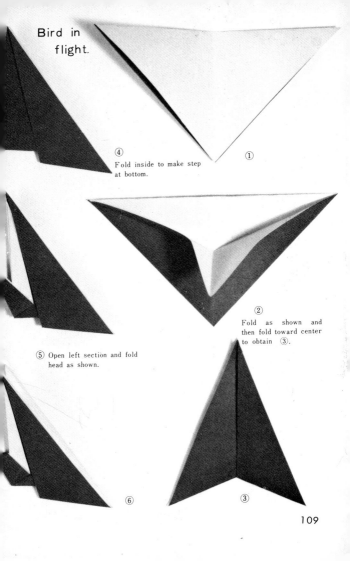

Bird in flight.

①

④ Fold inside to make step at bottom.

② Fold as shown and then fold toward center to obtain ③.

⑤ Open left section and fold head as shown.

⑥

③

109

Iris

① Fold to make triangle and fold again to make creases as shown.

②

③

④

⑤

⑤

②

⑤

③

⑥

④

Make two, one with color side uppermost and other with plain side uppermost.
Put one inside the other.

110

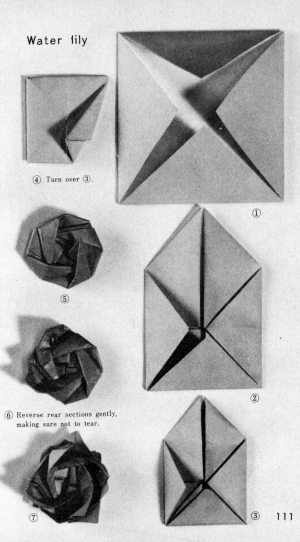

Water lily

④ Turn over ③.

⑤

⑥ Reverse rear sections gently, making sure not to tear.

⑦

①

②

③ 111

Crane-shaped receptacle

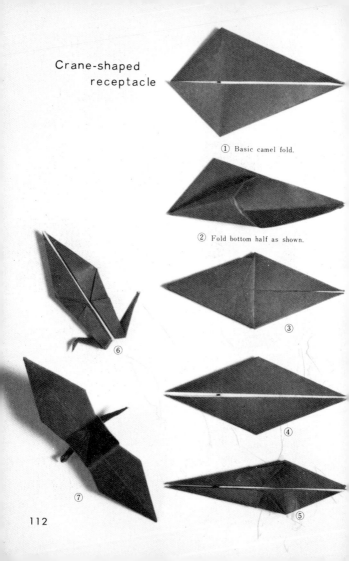

① Basic camel fold.

② Fold bottom half as shown.

③

④

⑤

⑥

⑦

Rocket

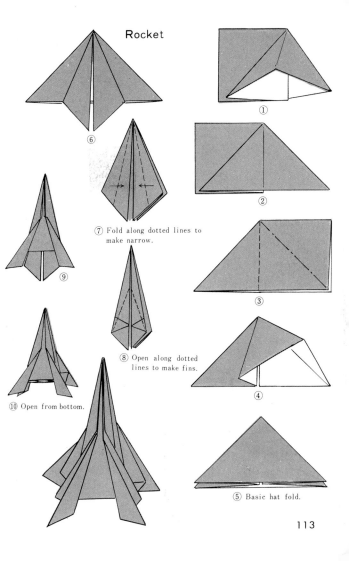

①

②

③

④

⑤ Basic hat fold.

⑥

⑦ Fold along dotted lines to make narrow.

⑧ Open along dotted lines to make fins.

⑨

⑩ Open from bottom.

113

Baby

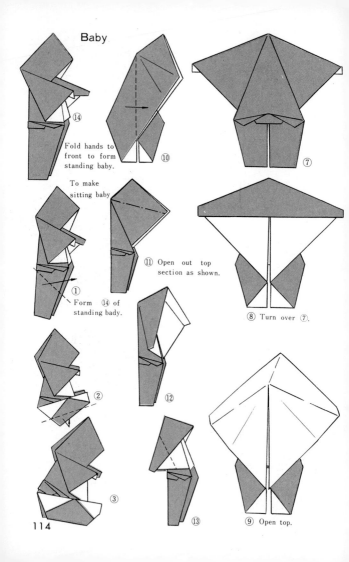

⑭

Fold hands to front to form standing baby.

To make sitting baby

① Form ⑭ of standing baby.

②

③

114

⑩

⑪ Open out top section as shown.

⑫

⑬

⑦

⑧ Turn over ⑦.

⑨ Open top.

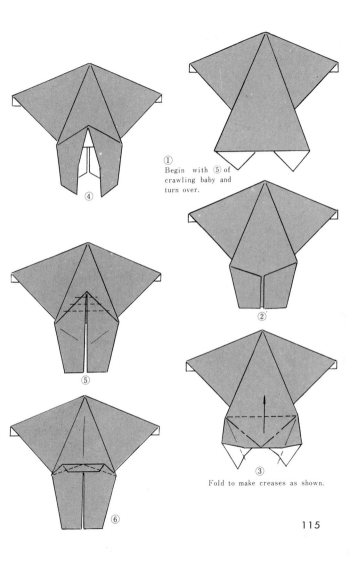

① Begin with ⑤ of crawling baby and turn over.

②

③

Fold to make creases as shown.

④

⑤

⑥

115

Goldfish mobile

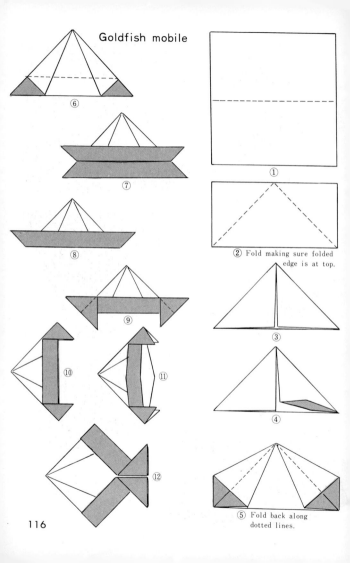

⑥

⑦

⑧

⑨

⑩

⑪

⑫

①

② Fold making sure folded edge is at top.

③

④

⑤ Fold back along dotted lines.

116

Ornamental ball

④

⑤

⑥

①

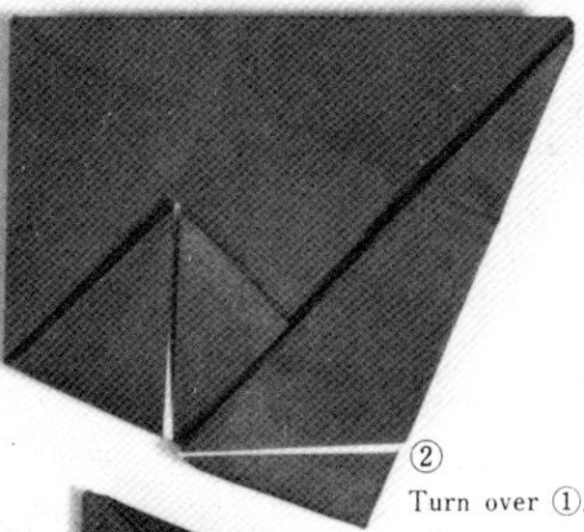

②

Turn over ①.

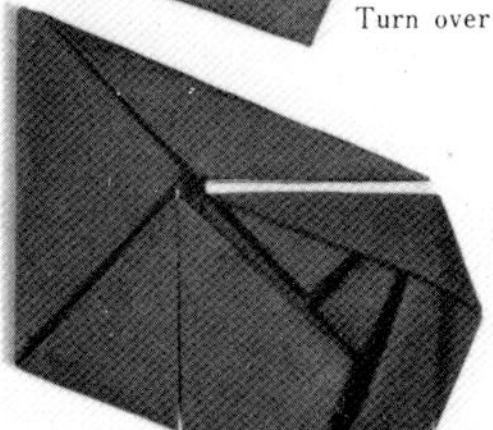

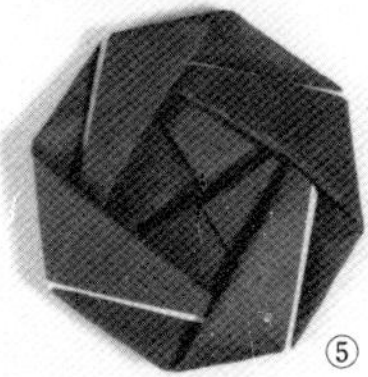

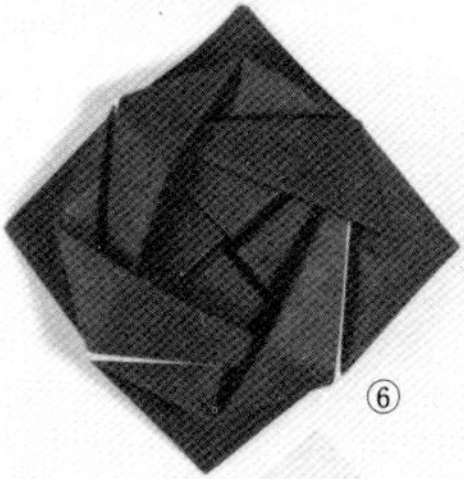

③

⑦ Make six in different colors and stick together to make ball.

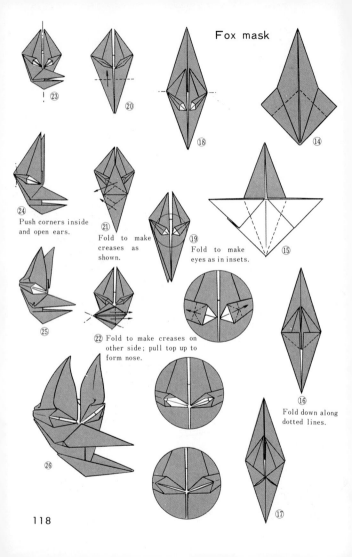

Fox mask

㉓

⑳

⑱

⑭

㉔ Push corners inside and open ears.

㉑ Fold to make creases as shown.

⑲ Fold to make eyes as in insets.

⑮

㉕

㉒ Fold to make creases on other side; pull top up to form nose.

⑯

Fold down along dotted lines.

㉖

⑰

118

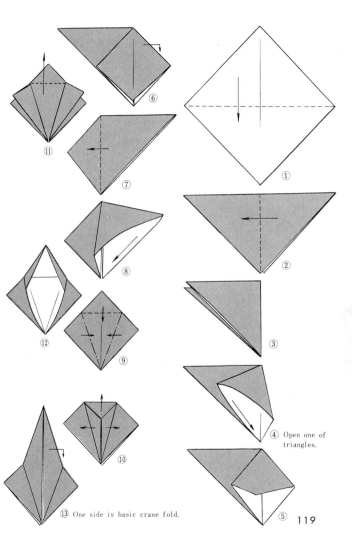

④ Open one of triangles.

⑬ One side is basic crane fold.

119

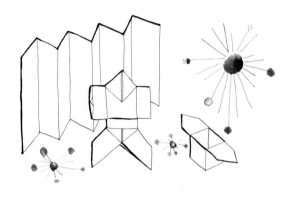

Basic forms

Countless figures can be made after memorizing origami's basic forms. The basic forms themselves, however, have various names and are approached differently depending on the school. I call the forms "crane," "hat" and so forth, but they can be given different names. The basic forms have already been introduced in the photographs, and the following pages show how to fold these forms. Some of the many shapes that can be made from the basic forms are listed below.

- From the basic crane fold: horse, elephant, cow, reindeer, monkey, bear, lion, cocker spaniel, standing crane, raven, Java sparrow, dragonfly, grasshopper, flamingo, female demon's mask, Buddha's mask, pharaoh's mask, praying man, others.
- From the basic hat fold: gorilla, sombrero, flower, frog, Tokyo Tower, starfish, sea turtle, others.
- From the basic camel fold: giraffe, rabbit, kangaroo, donkey, squirrel, sheep, reindeer, antelope, Dumbo the elephant, swan, parakeet, carp, crane-shaped receptacle, death mask, others.
- From the basic pony fold: jumping pony, lantern, hydrangea, mask for Chinese opera, others.

Lizards as well as dinosaurs can be made from the basic dinosaur fold, while rays and turtles come from the basic turtle fold. Birds in flight, jet planes and kites all derive from the same basic form. Goldfish and cowboy hats can also be made from the same basic fold. It is not difficult to discover new basic folds for use in many figures.

The folding sequences for the basic forms appear in a series of diagrams. The basic forms are explained in the following pages and not in the first part of this book. The reader should study the basic forms carefully in order to derive the maximum pleasure from origami.

Crane base (1)

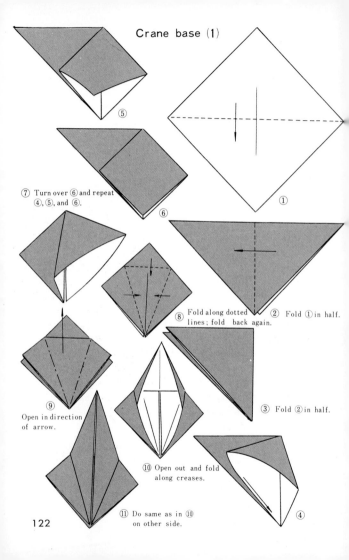

⑤

⑥

⑦ Turn over ⑥ and repeat ④, ⑤, and ⑥.

①

② Fold ① in half.

⑧ Fold along dotted lines; fold back again.

③ Fold ② in half.

⑨ Open in direction of arrow.

⑩ Open out and fold along creases.

⑪ Do same as in ⑩ on other side.

④

122

Crane base (2)

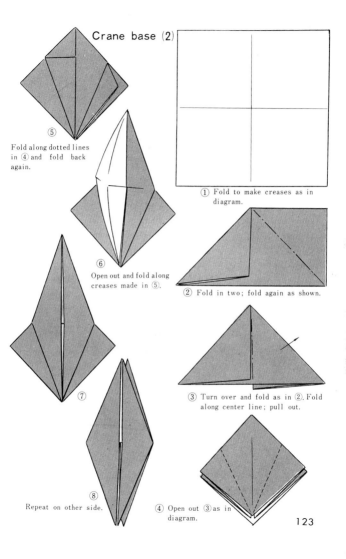

⑤ Fold along dotted lines in ④ and fold back again.

⑥ Open out and fold along creases made in ⑤.

⑦

⑧ Repeat on other side.

① Fold to make creases as in diagram.

② Fold in two; fold again as shown.

③ Turn over and fold as in ②. Fold along center line; pull out.

④ Open out ③ as in diagram.

123

Method of making pentagon

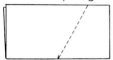

① Fold along dotted lines.

② Fold and make angles in ratio of 1:2.

③ Fold along dotted line in ②. Fold back along dotted line in ③.

④

Turn over ③. Cut at right-angles to edge along line. Open out to form pentagon.

124

Camel base

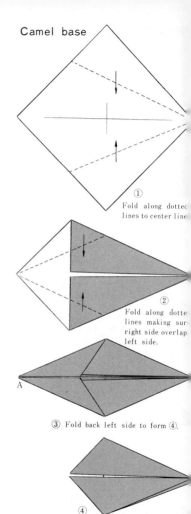

①
Fold along dotted lines to center line.

②
Fold along dotted lines making sure right side overlap left side.

③ Fold back left side to form ④.

A

④

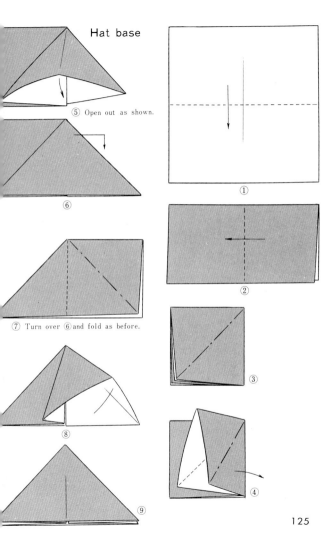

Hat base

①

②

③

④

⑤ Open out as shown.

⑥

⑦ Turn over ⑥ and fold as before.

⑧

⑨

125

Turtle base

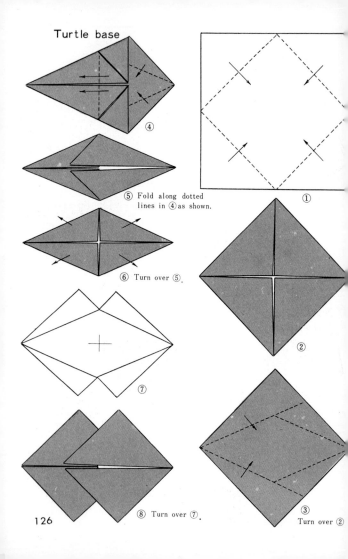

④

⑤ Fold along dotted lines in ④ as shown.

⑥ Turn over ⑤.

⑦

⑧ Turn over ⑦.

①

②

③
Turn over ②.

126

Dinosaur base

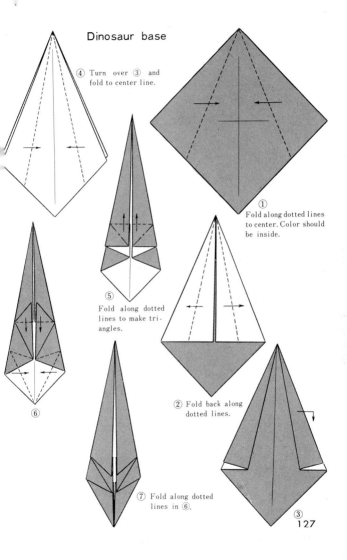

④ Turn over ③ and fold to center line.

① Fold along dotted lines to center. Color should be inside.

② Fold back along dotted lines.

③

⑤ Fold along dotted lines to make triangles.

⑥

⑦ Fold along dotted lines in ⑥.

127

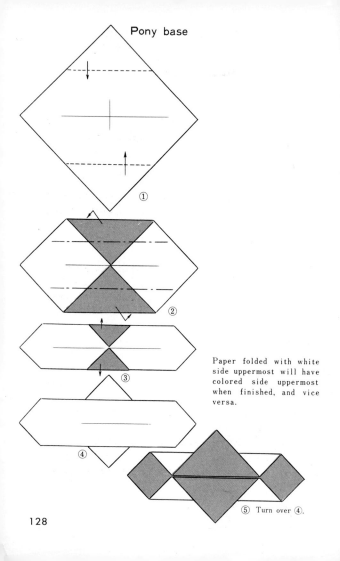

Pony base

①

②

③

④

⑤ Turn over ④.

Paper folded with white side uppermost will have colored side uppermost when finished, and vice versa.

128

Creative Origami

Traditional and Creative Origami

Traditional origami is represented by the crane, *yakko-san* (servant) and a boat which changes its shape by manipulation. Children learn all these from their parents. But when a person puts new ideas to work and devises new forms he is working in creative origami.

In traditional origami the same result could always be obtained if there was a diagram to follow. In creative origami, however, different shapes are possible even when the same thing is made because the finished work bears the stamp of the folder's personality.

This is especially so in a mask. The folder's character and emotions appear to be delicately expressed in the work. It is strange that the size of the eyes and mouth and the length of the nose are never the same, and that every mask has a different expression. One characteristic of creative origami is that the individual's ability clearly marks his work.

Increase Your Observation

In order to make birds and animals with origami, you must know their shape, movements and habits, otherwise a dog will not look like a dog and a sparrow will not resemble a sparrow.

When you make a mask there is always a difference in the facial expression whether you know the mask's history and legend or not. When you make Noh and other masks from drama, you may lose half the enjoyment of folding if you do not know the drama and the particular character. For creative origami, too, you need an extensive general knowledge. One must keenly observe and study the object he wants to make. The main points of creative origami are beauty and faithfulness to actual form.

Tools are not Necessary

We use the words "carve" for sculpture and "paint" for painting but we say "fold" for origami. We need instruments for the former two activities but none for the latter. Fingers are all one needs for origami, but they must be trained.

A sheet of paper contains unlimited "invisible" lines to fold from which we must choose the correct lines for making a desired shape. Whether the paper is folded correctly or not depends solely on the folder's skill.

Beauty of Form in Origami

There are certain points essential for bringing out the beauty in origami.

When we treat origami as an art, we need a delicate sensitivity even in the simplest folding action. Identical figures folded by different persons reflect the different personalities of the folders. Thus, it is important for the folder to strive for this sensitivity and to develop a sense for his material's qualities and color. One must choose the size, thickness, color and quality of paper that best fits what he intends to make.

It is not incorrect to use complicated methods when creating origami figures but it is better to use simple folding methods to obtain more realistic forms. I hope that everyone who attempts to create origami figures will observe certain principles, and study ways to express beauty in their work.

Principles of Creative Origami

A group I established for studying creative origami forbids the use of scissors on principle. Abiding by this rule of enjoyment creative origami became twofold. If you use scissors too freely, origami approaches too closely to the art of cutting paper to make various shapes. Productions lack creativity because of the shortcuts scissors introduce. This does not mean scissors should be ruled out completely. Primarily, however, they should be used solely to make incisions for gaining better effects. No part of the paper should be cut off. In classical origami scissors were used to make the thousand cranes, but only incisions were made.

Compound forms

Certain origami figures require more than one sheet of paper. Before you introduce scissors to obtain the real shape of what you are making, try using two or more sheets of paper to make different parts and then join them. When two or more parts are joined to make a figure it is called a compound form.

The grasshopper, with its raised forelegs, triangular face and wings, is one such form. It is impossible to make a grasshopper using one sheet of square paper, although it can be made from one sheet of triangular paper. In this book I demonstrated folding a grasshopper with two sheets of paper:

one for the face, forelegs and wings, and the other for the remaining legs and the rear half of the body.

Some animals are made by folding the front and rear halves separately. A combination of a mask and a person requires three sheets of paper: one for the mask, another for the upper half of the body and the third for the lower half of the body. With two sheets of paper you can make Buddhist images, Pan, the Japanese gods of wind and thunder or beautiful nudes.

Invitation to Creative Origami

I recommend that beginners memorize all the basic forms and study carefully how to develop the figure desired. One should observe in real life what one wants to make to grasp the correct shape and character. It is a good idea to study using a picture book or an art book.

Two or three questions would quickly test your power of observation. Do you know, for example, that a whale's tail extends horizontally not vertically? Do you know a chimpanzee holds its arms up while an orangutan lets them dangle? It is important to use your eyes all the time, and to sketch the shape of things in your mind. After mastering realism you can then make your work more symbolic and abstract. The classical origami crane has a formal beauty that is not merely a copy of a real crane.

Intensive research into the crane's formal beauty determined that the classical fold was most fitting. The crane is origami's greatest masterpiece and is readily understood by the present generation. Foreigners immediately associate the classical crane with origami.

When you do research into origami symbolization and abstraction, an acute creative sense and keen observation are helpful. In order to develop these senses, one should study art, sculpture and flower arrangements.

There are special difficulties in making masks. A mask should express joy or anger but will not if paper is only folded twenty or thirty times. When the sculptor makes a Noh mask he applies his whole heart and soul to his work. The artist must likewise apply himself to capture the delicate expression in an origami mask.

It is easy to enter the world of creative origami, but creativity is profound. I hope you enjoy this world and will contribute your own ideas to make it richer.

The Educational Value of Creative Origami

Children who merely copy how to fold origami do not reap any great educational benefit. It appears simple to make an origami figure using a sheet of paper and nothing else, but, on the contrary, it needs a highly creative sense.

Whereas painting needs a canvas and sculpture needs space, origami needs only a sheet of paper. In the sheet of paper, however, exist endless folding possibilities. To make origami forms one must have the insight to see the paper's "invisible" lines in order to fold and produce something. Moreover, while other arts depend on brushes, paint, chisels and other tools or media, the fingers make all kinds of origami shapes and forms. Actually, the person who disagrees with the role origami can play in formative education probably lacks a true understanding of the art.

Problems exist, too, in teaching origami. Children taught established ways of folding, for example, adopt a passive attitude. Moreover, children who learn fast tend to feel superior when they quickly memorize a sequence while children who experience difficulty in folding paper correctly or following directions become depressed. Origami taught that way stifles creativity instead of nurturing it.

Children should learn how to fold paper correctly but should not be taught that only by folding in a certain way can such and such an animal or object be made. If the teaching method is correct, origami becomes a most convenient educational material.

Origami seems to be better understood today, and is used

more often in kindergartens and nurseries. Teachers who use origami in kindergartens find the children so enthusiastic that they forget the time.

Children surprise themselves by making various shapes without cutting the paper. Their favorites are squirrels, penguins and elephants. Children seem to see something magical in origami.

It is possible to make forms quickly, using many colors and without taking up much space. Children realize their dreams by producing many figures they can play with afterwards. Children tend to enjoy producing various figures when they realize they are creating "playmates."